MOTHERLY POEMS OF WISDOM

By: Lillie C. Gattis

Motherly Poems of Wisdom
By: Lillie C. Gattis

Cover Design By: Anelda L. Ballard/Jameel Hobbins
Cover Photograph By: Lillie C. Gattis/Jameel Hobbins

Logo Designs By: Andre M. Saunders and Leroy Grayson
Editor: Editing Solutions
Assistant Editor: Anelda L. Ballard
Photographs By: Lillie C. Gattis, www.photobucket.com, www.freefoto.com, www.randallsmith.com, www.webcrawler.com, www.puttingjesusfirst.com www.homeboyastronomy.com

© 2010 Lillie C. Gattis
ISBN 978-0-9843255-3-5
ISBN 0-9843255-3-0
Library of Congress Control Number: 2010925015

All rights reserved. This book is protected under the copyright laws of the United States of America. This book may not be copied or reprinted for commercial gain or profit. The use of short quotations or occasional page copying for personal or group study is permitted and encouraged. Permission will be granted upon request. Unknown author poems are from the internet.

For Worldwide Distribution. Printed in the United States of America
Published by Jazzy Kitty Greetings Marketing & Publishing, LLC
Utilizing Microsoft and Adobe Publishing Software.

ACKNOWLEDGMENTS

I want to first and foremost thank God, Our Father, and Our Lord and Savior Jesus Christ for His love, grace and mercy towards me and all of those that believed in me and my endeavor in this project.

I would like to acknowledge my mother Mrs. Eva Cottingham and my Aunt Annie Briscoe for their prayers and love, who are both deceased. My brother Mr. George Cottingham and Sister-in-Law Mrs. Eleanor Cottingham who have both been like a mother and father to me.

My Pastor Dr. Kenneth Porter and, my church family that have prayed for me. Also, my former pastor, Bishop W. Weeks Sr. and first lady where I first received my salvation.

My supervisor Mrs. Diane Carrol, who inspired me, by just being in her presence and for introducing me to Mr. Edward Parker, who introduced me to this great publisher Evangelist Anelda Ballard and her husband Reverend Ronald Ballard Jr., who are both a Godly inspiration to me.

To all my brothers and sisters, my children, grand children and great granddaughter who never gave up in believing in me.

May God continue to bless each one with His richest blessings and abundant life. These are the people I have the greatest honor and respect for.

Many thanks to Sister Polly Hall-Gibbs for the time that she put in typing my first book project. May God continue to bless her.

Much Love and Prayers,
Author Lillie C. Gattis

DEDICATIONS

This collection of poems is dedicated foremost to my Lord and Savior, Jesus Christ; my mother, the late Eva Cottingham, my natural and spiritual families and most of all to my Pastor, Apostle Kenneth Porter.

I thank God through the inspiration of the Holy Spirit for giving me this gift of writing; which is long overdue in sharing it and spreading it abroad to others.

Some of these poems were written prior to me receiving Christ in my life but will inspire your soul for years to come.

Author Lillie C. Gattis

TABLE OF CONTENTS

INTRODUCTION i

  CHAPTER 1 – PERSONAL SENTIMENT POEMS 01

    In My World 03
    What Does Carmen Mean to Me? 05
    Thanks for Caring, George & Eleanor 07
    Look Up 09
    Life is Worthwhile 11
    Knowledge of Life 13
    Souls 15
    A Mothers Love 18

  CHAPTER 2 – LOVE POEMS 19

    The Love of My Life 21
    You'll Always Be in My Heart 22

  CHAPTER 3 – INSPIRED BY THE BIBLE 23

    Concepts from Psalm 103 25
    Psalm 107 27
    Witness to a Soul 29
    Who is This Baby? 30

  CHAPTER 4 – POEMS WRITTEN BY OTHERS 31

    In Daddy's Steps 33
    My Master and I 36
    The Man in the Mirror 39

TABLE OF CONTENTS

- **CHAPTER 5 – POEMS WITH HOLIDAY THOUGHTS** 40
  - Stranger 42
  - What is Easter? 45
- **CHAPTER 6 – COLLECTIBLE POEMS** 46
  - Black Man Hold On 47
  - A Virtuous Woman 48
  - Do You Hear What I Hear 51
  - Thank You Lord 53
  - When I'm an Old Lady 55
- **CHAPTER 7 – POEMS DEDICATED TO LOVE ONES** 58
  - The Man, The Ministry, The Vision 60
  - Daughter & Granddaughters 61
  - Brothers "Jamil & Andrew" 63
  - Latisha 65
  - Ryesha 67
- **ABOUT THE AUTHOR** 68

INTRODUCTION

This collection of poems were written with you in mind. God has given me this gift to inspire, uplift and encourage you in your day by day life.

This God given gift has blessed me to reach those of all ages. These poems were written for family members, men, women, children, for the hopeless, non-Christians and Christians alike. They will encourage you for years to come.

Once you start reading this book, you won't want to put it down. It will make you think, laugh and even cry.

After reading this book you will be left with an impression to love more, appreciate and uplift your family, friends and all those you meet.

From an Author's Heart
Lillie C. Gattis

CHAPTER 1

PERSONAL SENTIMENT POEMS

- In My World
- What Does Carmen Mean to Me?
- Thanks for Caring George & Eleanor
- Look Up!
- Life is Worthwhile
- Knowledge of Life
- Souls
- A Mothers Love

IN MY WORLD

In my world lies a goal

And it's embedded deep down in my soul.

I've longed to reach this goal you see

And you can bet,

It means the world to me.

IN MY WORLD

In my world lies a goal
And it's embedded deep down in my soul.

I've longed to reach this goal you see
And you can bet,
It means the world to me.

For I'm an individual who finishes his race
And never gives up,
No matter the pace.

For living a full life is my dream and whoever joins,
We'll be a team.

CARMEN

WHAT DOES "CARMEN" MEAN TO ME?

WHAT DOES "CARMEN" MEAN TO ME?

C is for the COURAGE that I can see in you

A is for ALERT in all that you do

R is for READY to follow your star

M is for MATURE you already are

E is for EAGER to accomplish your dream

N is FOR NEW your new life will begin

CARMEN,

I HAVE LOVED YOU FROM BEGINNING TO END

May God Bless You Always,

With many more Birthdays!

Love You!

~ Mom

THANKS FOR CARING
GEORGE & ELEANOR

FOR YOU TWO HAVE BEEN A BLESSING
FROM THE VERY START
AND THE LOVE I HAVE FOR YOU BOTH,
COMES RIGHT FROM MY HEART

THANKS FOR CARING
GEORGE & ELEANOR

Sometimes, I sit and wonder what life would be like
If it wasn't for you brother, and if it wasn't for your wife.

For you two have been a blessing from the very start
And the love I have for you both, comes right from my heart.

For a family is giving, and also caring too
And that description of a family fits the both of you.

For it's never been a time that you did not give a hand,
To some boy or some girl and also for a woman or man.

Yes, I can truly say that people like you are few;
People that hold out a helping hand, and do the things you do.

For I might not have silver or gold to give you for pay.
Yet, I can ask God for mercy for you each and every day.

So as I close this poem that I've dedicated to you
My prayers and love for you is eternal
And they are given faithfully from me to you.

From Your Sister and Your Sister-In-Law

LOOK UP!

MY CHILDREN, GRANDCHILDREN, AND GREAT GRANDDAUGHTER

LOOK UP!

Look up to life wherever you are
And Never be afraid to follow that star
For life for you will be no easy road Because you are human
You will have to carry the load
Sometimes you might have to shed a few tears

But keep God Number "1" and He'll always be near
I won't be around always for you
But with my Father above
You'll know what to do

For life can be beautiful for you to see
Because of Jesus - It has for me

But "never" stop short of reaching your goal
And do what God would have you to;

And you will live to grow old, full of wisdom, knowledge and grace
For you didn't give up but you ran the whole race.

With Love Always! ~**Mom**

Dedicated to My Children, Grandchildren, and Great Granddaughter:

Vanessa, Zadine, Jamil, Andrew, Carmen, Ryesha, Latisha, Avery, Elijah, Karin, Maxwell, and Morgan

LIFE IS WORTHWHILE

BUT SEARCH AND LEARN ALL YOU CAN

AND GET TO KNOW YOUR FELLOW MAN

FOR IF YOU GET DOWN,

YOU WILL ALWAYS HAVE A HAND

AND THEY WILL COME TO YOUR AID

LIKE PEBBLES IN THE SAND

LIFE IS WORTHWHILE

Life is worthwhile wherever you go
With wisdom and knowledge and your desire to know

Sometimes life seems it's only a play
And we are only players living "day by day"

But if we will remember we have God up above
And when you've Got Him, you've also got His love

It might seem hard to live in this world with troubles,
Trials and test
But be of good courage and keep your head up
For you can only do your best

You might be young, with a lot of searching to do
And want to know more

But search and learn all you can
And get to know your fellow man
For if you get down,
You will always have a hand

And they will come to your aid like pebbles in the sand
For this is only a small message my friend
So love and be friendly as much as you can.

KNOWLEDGE OF LIFE

SATAN ALWAYS HAD A GAME…

HE'S WAY OF THINKING IS ALWAYS THE SAME

YOUR LIFE CAN BE FREE AS A BIRD

BUT SATAN WILL

MAKE IT WHATEVER HE FEELS

AND WHAT HE DOESN'T GET, HE WILL STEAL

KNOWLEDGE OF LIFE

SATAN always had a game…
He's way of thinking is always the same
Your life can be free as a bird

But SATAN will
Make it whatever he feels
And what he doesn't get, he will steal

Your heart, your mind and try to take your soul,
For he doesn't care, he is bold

Knowledge comes from God above
You can overcome with His love

For if you are weak, He will use that too
To do the things He wants to do

Through God's love, you can stand
And use these tools against SATAN'S band.

SOULS

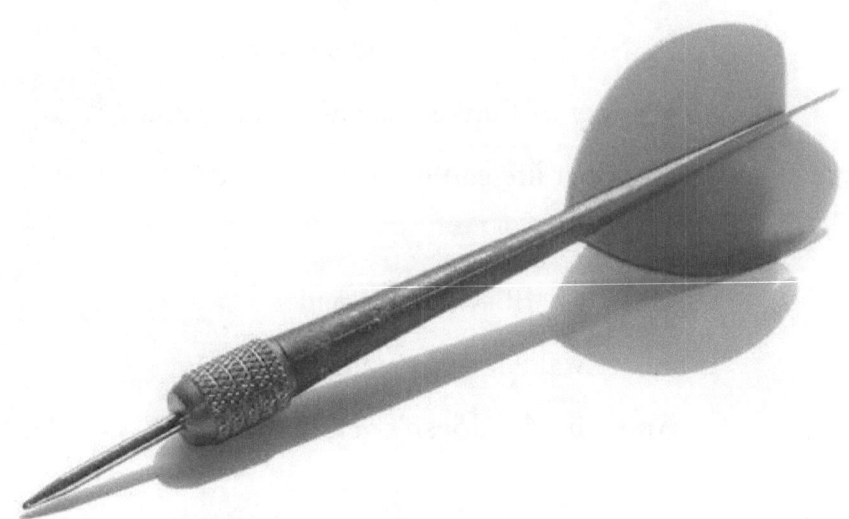

AS I SEARCH WITHIN MY HEART
I FEEL THIS BURDEN LIKE A DART,
THAT PIERCES BY SOUL DEEP WITHIN

BECAUSE I ALSO WAS LOST IN SIN
AND FELT THERE
WAS NO HOPE AROUND
A SOUL LOST BUT NOW I AM FOUND

SOULS

How can I forget the people I meet
As they travel up and down the street?
Some are lost and can't find their way,
As they go about day by day.

As I search within my heart
I feel this burden like a dart,
That pierces by soul deep within
Because I also was lost in sin
And felt there was no hope around
A soul lost but now I am found.

For Jesus came and set me free
For I was surely in captivity.
Now as I look at others like me,
I say to myself, they too can be set free!

That God above loves them as well
And does not want their souls in Hell.

(Continued)

SOULS

But who can reach these souls today?
Where do you start? What do you say?

For so many Christians have lived a lie -
These souls are looking and wondering why?

They say they are saved and set free
But they are living like they are lost at sea.

And so that soul sinks deeper still
Because the hope they had we also killed.

So what does a soul mean to you?
Are you willing to do all that you can do?

To keep that soul from being lost
You and I must count the cost!

Forget the things you want to do
But love a soul, like God loves you.

A MOTHER'S LOVE

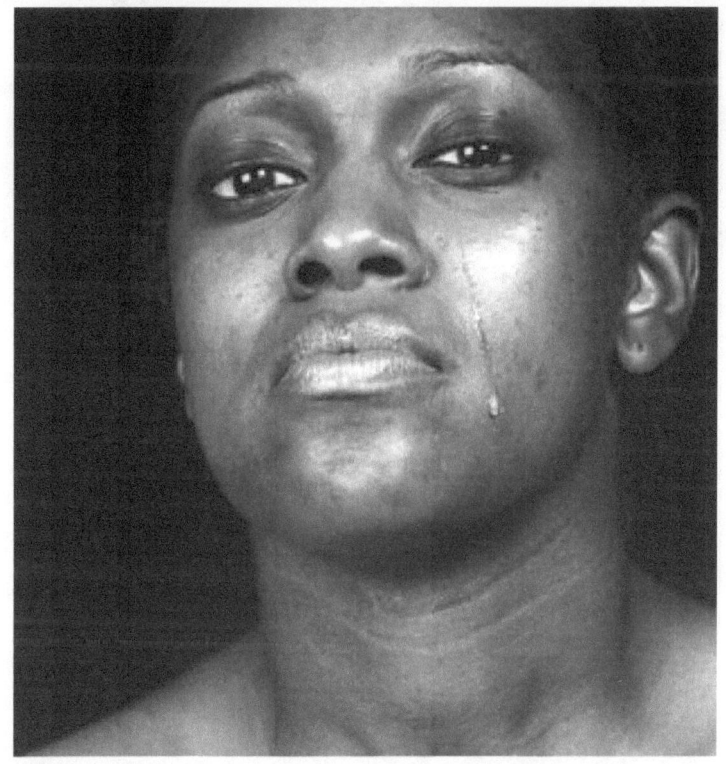

I SAW YOUR MOTHER, YOUR FRIEND MAY SAY,
AND AS I APPROACHED HER – SHE WALKED AWAY.
YOU SEE, SHE HAD BEEN CRYING ABOUT YOU,
AND THE LOOK IN HER EYES,
SAID SHE DIDN'T KNOW WHAT TO DO

THAT SHOWS HOW DEEP IS HER LOVE
BECAUSE IT IS PLANTED
BY THE MASTER UP ABOVE

A MOTHER'S LOVE

I saw your mother, your friend may say,

And as I approached her – she walked away.

You see, she had been crying about you,

And the look in her eyes, said she didn't know what to do

That shows how deep is her love

Because it is planted by the Master up above

Some people may say things about your kids

You still love them – after all of what they did

It's a bond – deep you see

And that love is given to you and to me

Some mothers will walk through a fire

For their children

That mother's love is what you have to admire.

So on **Mother's Day** – Thank God above

For it you have a good mother

You have pure love!

CHAPTER 2
LOVE POEMS

- The Love of My Life
- You'll Always Be in My Heart!

THE LOVE OF MY LIFE

IT WAS TIMES, I WASN'T TRUE,
GOING IN CIRCLES
NOT KNOWING WHAT TO DO

YOU WERE ALWAYS THERE
THROUGH THICK AND THIN
STILL LOVING ME,
NO MATTER WHAT I DID
OR NO MATTER WHERE I'D BEEN

THE LOVE OF MY LIFE

Dear JESUS,

There are not many people in life that's true,
That's why I am in love with You.

I tried to love others from my heart,
But it was a failure from the very start.

Then I met You one day long ago,
Although I was messed up, You didn't let go.

It was times, I wasn't true,
Going in circles not knowing what to do.

You were always there through thick and thin.
Still loving me,
No matter what I did or no matter where I'd been.

The Love of my life, my King and my Friend.
I will never let You go, but love You to the end.

YOU'LL ALWAYS BE IN MY HEART!

My precious black man, You stand so tall
You are an original the best of all

You're such a precious jewel to me
I opened my heart and gave you the key

You see I have a love divine
And a personality that's ever so kind
But sometimes fate speaks to you
And tells you the things you have to do

You see my flesh wants to stay
But deep down within, I must go away

I'll always cherish those moments with you,
But I know this is something I have to do

So stay sweet my precious, whatever you do
And whoever you choose, make sure they love you.

CHAPTER 3

POEMS INSPIRED BY THE BIBLE

- Concepts from Psalm 103
- Psalm 107
- Witness to a Soul
- Who is This Baby?

CONCEPTS FROM PSALM 103

The Blessings of the Lord

HE FORGAVE YOU ALL YOUR SINS
AND LET A NEW LIFE BEGIN
HE ALSO HEALS DISEASES –
TO ALL THOSE HE PLEASES

WHO KEEPS US FROM HARM,
WITH HIS TENDER AND GENTLE ARMS
WHO KEEPS US FROM SPEAKING EVIL
SO OUR YOUTH IS RENEWED LIKE THE EAGLE

CONCEPTS FROM PSALM 103
The Blessings of the Lord

Bless His Holy Name for this is where MERCY came.

His benefits too; for they come from Him to You

He forgave you all your sins and let a new life begin

He also heals diseases - to all those he pleases

Who keeps us from harm, with His tender and gentle arms

Who keeps us from speaking evil

So our youth is renewed like the eagle

He is fair in His judgment

And brings righteousness to the oppressed

Whether they are just or unjust

He gives nothing less

He made known His ways unto Moses of old,

And all the children of Israel untold

The Lord is merciful and gracious to you

And holds back His anger from some of the things we do

(Continued)

CONCEPTS FROM PSALM 103
The Blessings of the Lord

He will not always scold us for the wrong we do
Oh! How merciful He is to me and to you

He has not rewarded us for our sin
For He understands the life that we've been in
For as high as the heaven is above the earth,
So great is His mercy toward the children of men

As far as the east is from the west
He has removed our transgression and gave love,
His best Like a father - He pitieth us,
For He remembers that we are yet dust.

For this is why I love Him so,
And what He has done for me,
Only my Father knows.

PSALM 107

O Give Thanks Unto The Lord
For His Mercy Endureth Forever
O Give Thanks Unto The Lord
For all He has done for you

For without Him on your side
There is nothing you can do
He keeps you from harm everyday
No matter what you do or say

He blesses the good ones and the wrong
Because His love for all is strong
And His mercy is out of sight!
It can't be gained through power or might

He keeps your enemies far away
And allow you to see a brighter day.

O that men would praise His name,
His love for you will remain the same
He brought you out of darkness still
And He did it all on Calvary's hill
This is why I bless His name
Because with His Love - Mercy came!

WITNESS TO A SOUL

DID JESUS LOVE THEM TOO?
THAT ANSWER IS GIVEN TO ME AND YOU

JUST TO TELL THEM THAT HE IS JUST
AND THAT HE LOVES THEM NO MATTER
WHO THEY ARE
IN HIS EYESIGHT, THEY ARE A STAR

WITNESS TO A SOUL

Have you talked to a soul today?
As you traveled along your way?

Maybe they were walking by,
Looking up and wondering why?

Why had life cheated them so,
A question without an answer that they really didn't know.

Did Jesus love them too?
That answer is given to me and you.

Just to tell them that He is just
And that He loves them no matter who they are
In His eyesight, they are a star

Letting them know that it's never too late
And He is waiting for a date

To give their life to Him alone
And He will love them and take them home

WHO IS THIS BABY?

Who is this baby born over 2,000 years ago?
Who came into this world and set it aglow!

For it was prophesied by the prophet Isaiah
That He would be born and it would be told
That He would save all, the young and the old.

A wonderful Savior, Jesus is His name
And to see this Christ child that had no fame
To grow up to be hated and treated so bad
But besides that this lad, had no dad

For God Almighty was His Father you see,
And this Son would die and then get the key
To unlock our hearts and not only that
But to conquer death and hell - that is a fact.

So this Christmas, give Jesus your heart
Don't wait too late
For tomorrow is not promised to you
So save your own soul
Whatever you do!

CHAPTER 4

POEMS WRITTEN BY OTHERS

- In Daddy's Steps
- My Master and I
- The Man in the Mirror

IN DADDY'S STEPS

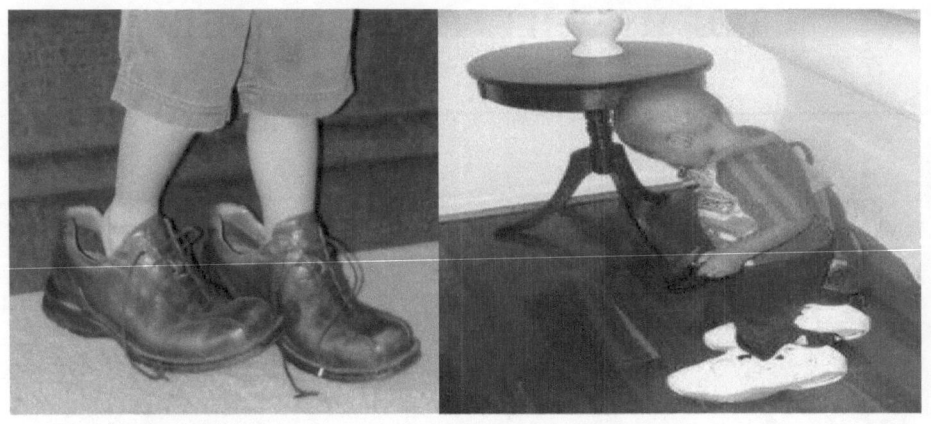

I WONDERED WHY A CHILD WOULD CHOOSE
TO WEAR HIS DAD'S OLD WORN-OUT SHOES?

I HEAR HIM SAY HIS VOICE SO GLAD,
"I WANT TO BE JUST LIKE MY DAD"

I HOPE HIS DAD - HIS STEPS WOULD CHOOSE,
SAFE FOR HIS SON TO WEAR HIS SHOES

IN DADDY'S STEPS

I watched him playing around my door,
My neighbor's little boy of four.

I wondered why a child would choose
To wear his dad's old worn-out shoes?

I saw him try with all his might
To make the laces snug and tight
I smiled to see him walk and then
He'd only step right out again.

I hear him say his voice so glad,
"I want to be just like my dad"

I hope his dad - his steps would choose,
Safe for his son to wear his shoes.

And then a shout and cry of joy,
A "Hello, Dad!" and a "Hi-You, Boy!"
They walked along in measured stride
Each face aglow with love and pride.

(Continued)

IN DADDY'S STEPS

"What have you done today, my lad?"
"I tried to wear your old shoes, Dad
They are big but when I am a man,
I'll wear your shoes, I know I can."

They stopped and stood there hand-in-hand.
He saw his son's tracks in the sand.
His words - A Prayer - came back to me.
"Lord, let my steps lead him to Thee."

~Author Unknown

MY MASTER AND I

THIS POEM IS DEDICATED TO
THE LATE ANDREW M. CLAYTON SR.
KNOW AS BROTHER J.

MY MASTER AND I

I had walked life's path with an easy tread:
Had followed where pleasure and. comfort lead:
And then by chance, in a quiet place,
I met the Master, Face to face.

With station and rank and wealth for a goal,
Much thought for the body, but none for the soul.
I had entered to win in life's mad race,
When I met the Master, Face to face.

I had built my castles, and had reared them high,
Until their towers had pierced the blue of the sky;
I had sworn to rule with iron mace
When I met the Master, Face to face

I met Him, and I knew Him, and I blushed to see
That His eyes full of sorrow were fixed on me;

(Continued)

MY MASTER AND I

And I faltered and fell at His feet that day,
While my castles melted and vanished away.

Melted and vanished, and in their place,
I could see naught else but my Master's face,
I cried aloud, "Oh, make me meek
To follow the marks of thy wounded feet."

My thought is now for the souls of men;
I lost my life, to find it again,
Ever since in that quiet place
My Master and I stood face to face.

~Author Unknown

THE MAN IN THE MIRROR

THE MAN IN THE MIRROR IS LOOKING AT YOU
FOR HE HAS BEEN LOST
AND DIDN'T KNOW WHAT TO DO

FOR GOD HAS GIVEN HIM A NEW LIFE, YOU SEE
AND IF YOU CAN STAND,
GOD WILL GIVE YOU THE KEY

THE MAN IN THE MIRROR

The man in the mirror is looking at you
For he has been LOST and didn't know what to do.

For God has given him a NEW LIFE, you see
And if you can stand, God will give you THE KEY

To look inside your heart & mind, which is YOUR SOUL
For He is willing to give you a new life
So you can GROW OLD

For WISDOM is the principal thing for you
Especially in the times when you don't know what to do.

Your life has been no easy road,
But remember who held you and carried the LOAD.

For God know your life would be hard,
But He is the King and He held the CARDS
Maybe right now you don't understand
But when it's over, you'll see a new man.

For He is not through with you my DEAR FRIEND
But you will be complete if you give God the rest (of your life)
And in return…He will give you the BEST!

~ Lillie C. Gattis

CHAPTER 5
POEMS WITH HOLIDAY THOUGHTS

- Stranger
- What is Easter?

STRANGER

THE CHILDREN LEARN OF SANTA CLAUS
WHILE THEY ARE STILL QUITE SMALL
WHEN CHRISTMAS COMES
"HE" IS THE MOST "IMPORTANT" ONE OF ALL

THE STRANGER HUNG HIS HEAD IN SHAME,
HE CLOSED A NAIL PIERCED HAND;
HIS BODY SHOOK IN DISBELIEF –
HE DID NOT UNDERSTAND

BUT CLEAR, "AFTER ALL THESE YEARS
THEY STILL DON'T KNOW,"
AND JESUS SHED A TEAR

STRANGER

At Christmas time there was a man, who looked so out of place.
As people rushed about him, at a hurried pace.
He stared at all the Christmas lights, the tinsel everywhere.
The shopping center Santa Claus with children gathered near.

The mall was packed with shoppers, who were going to and fro.
Some with smiles, some with frowns, and some too tired to go.
They rested on benches, or they hurried on their way.
To fight the crowds for purchases, to carry home that day.

The music from the stereo, was playing loud and clear.
Of Santa Claus and snowmen, and funny nosed reindeer.

He heard the people talk about, the good times on the way.
Of parties, fun and food galore, and gift exchange that day.
I'd like to know what's going on; the man was heard to say.

There seems to be some sort, of celebration on the way.
And would you tell me who this is, all dressed in red and white.
And why are children asking "him" about a special night.

(Continued)

STRANGER

The answer came in disbelief,
I can't believe my ears.
I can't believe you do not know,
That Christmas time is here.

The time when Santa comes around
With gifts for girls and boys.
When they are asleep on Christmas Eve,
He leaves them books and toys.

The man you see in red and white
Is Santa Claus so sly.
The children love his joyful laugh
And twinkle in his eye.

His gift packed sleigh is pulled along,
By very small reindeer.
As he flies quickly through the air
While darting here and there.

(Continued)

STRANGER

The children learn of Santa Claus
While they are still quite small.
When Christmas comes
"he" is the most "important" one of all.

The stranger hung his head in shame,
He closed a nail pierced hand;
His body shook in disbelief - He did not understand.

A shadow crossed His stricken face,
His voice was low
But clear, "After all these years
They still don't know,"

And JESUS shed a tear.

~Author Unknown

WHAT IS EASTER?

E is for the ETERNAL LIFE that He gave.

A is for AFTER He rose from the grave.

S is for SALVATION so full and free.

T is for TOTAL LOVE - He has given to me.

E - is for ENTER into his rest.

R is FOR REALIZE God has given his best.

JESUS is His Son that He has given alone.
God sent him to Calvary so he could come home
To Save You from damnation, you see,
So this is what EASTER really means to me.

CHAPTER 6
COLLECTIBLE POEMS

- Black Man Hold On
- A Virtuous Woman
- Do You Hear What I Hear?
- Thank You Lord
- When I'm an Old Lady

BLACK MAN HOLD ON

Black man HOLD ON whatever you do
Be honest with yourself and God will see you through
Work on your mind, let it become new
Because it controls the heart, and all that it can do

You see, the brain is an organ so strong
With it you can think right or you can think wrong
Thoughts are only visions that turn into reality
And you can be in control of your destiny

Ways and actions can bring you hell
And you will feel like you're under a spell
But you have the strength to see your way through
And if you follow God's guidance, there is nothing you can't do

The Black Man is lost and out of control
And I pray for his unity and also for his soul.

A VIRTUOUS WOMAN

Who can find a virtuous woman?
For her price is far above rubies. Proverbs 31:10

The heart of her husband safety trust,
For doing him good, not just for the day,
But throughout his life all the way.

She worketh willingly with her hands,
And is always respected throughout the land.

(Continued)

A VIRTUOUS WOMAN

She purchases food and clothes for her family.
And is busy every day

She rises while it is night
To prepare for the day before the light.

She girdeth her loins and strengthens her arms,
And in her heart, she does no harm.

She stretches her hand to the poor.
And if she could she would do more.

Her husband is known throughout the gates.
For he is honored for a wonderful mate.

Her children arises and calls her blessed,
For God has given them, His absolutely best.

Favor is deceitful and beauty is vain,
But a women that fears the Lord,
Shall always be praised.

DO YOU HEAR WHAT I HEAR?

DO YOU HEAR WHAT I HEAR?
JESUS CHRIST IS CALLING YOU,
OUT OF THE DARKNESS, INTO HIS LIGHT

FOR IT'S NOT GOD YOU HAVE TO FIGHT
SHOWING YOU HIS LOVE THROUGH HIS WORD,
FROM THE BIBLE, I KNOW YOU HAVE HEARD

DO YOU HEAR WHAT I HEAR?

Do you Hear What I Hear?
A sound of music in the air

A time of unity and also love
That God has ordained from up above

Do you hear what I hear?

People are tired of being depressed
But want their minds at peace and rest

Do you hear what I hear?

Our youth are crying from within,
Trying to be women and also men.

Growing up too fast in such a short time,
Children that are yours, and also mine.

(Continued)

DO YOU HEAR WHAT I HEAR?

Many are saying they have the solution,
My God, we don't need a revolution

Do you hear what I hear?
Jesus Christ is calling you,
Out of the darkness, into His light

For it's not God you have to fight.
Showing you His love through His word,
From the Bible, I know you have heard.

So come my brothers and sisters too
For Jesus loves you and we do to.

THANK YOU LORD

Thank you Lord for blessing us,
You have given us mercy, because you are just.
Every day you let us wake up, its your grace,
To be able to see our love ones face to face.

It's amazing what you have done,
All people you bless, one by one.
When we are in trouble, you are there to see us through.
There is nothing for us you won't do

Thank you Lord, just for being you.
The greatest of great, our one and only King,
And because of you we can rejoice and sing.

WHEN I'M AN OLD LADY

WHEN I'M AN OLD LADY
I'LL LIVE WITH MY KIDS,
AND MAKE THEM SO HAPPY
JUST AS THEY DID

WHEN I'M AN OLD LADY

When I'm an Old Lady
I'll live with my kids,
And make them so happy
Just as they did

I want to pay back,
All the joy they've provided
Returning each deed
Oh, they'll be so excited
When I'm an Old Lady
And live with my kids.

I'll write on the walls with reds, whites and blues
And bounce on the furniture wearing my shoes.
I'll drink from the carton and then leave it out.
I'll stuff all the toilets and oh, how they'll shout!
When I'm an Old Lady
And live with my kids.

(Continued)

WHEN I'M AN OLD LADY

When they're on the phone and just out of reach,
I'll get into things like sugar and bleach

Oh, they'll snap their fingers
And then shake their head.
And when that is done,
I'll hide under the bed.
When I'm an Old Lady
And live with my kids.

When they cook dinner and call me to meals
I'll not eat my green beans or salads congealed.
I'll gag on my okra, spill milk on the table
And when they get angry, run fast as I'm able.
When I'm an Old Lady
And live with my kids.

I'll sit close to the TV, thru the channels I'll click
I'll cross both my eyes, to see if they stick.

(Continued)

WHEN I'M AN OLD LADY

I'll take off my socks and throw one away
And play in the mud until the end of the day
When I'm an Old Lady
And live with my kids.

And later in bed, I'll lay back and sigh
And thank God in prayer and then close my eyes
And my kids will look down with a smile slowly creeping
And say with a groan. "She's so sweet when she's sleeping."
When I'm an Old Lady
And live with my kids.

~Unknown Author

CHAPTER 7

POEMS DEDICATED TO LOVE ONES

- The Man, The Ministry, The Vision
- Daughter & Granddaughters
- Brothers "Jamil & Andrew"
- Latisha
- Ryesha

THE MAN, THE MINISTRY, THE VISION

TO PREACH THE WORD LOUD AND STRONG
NO MATTER WHAT THE WORLD WOULD SAY,
TO LEAD THE PEOPLE ALL THE WAY

THE MAN, THE MINISTRY, THE VISION

It happen a long time ago
When he was just a babe
God had a calling on his life
A charge the Master gave.

To preach the Word loud and strong
No matter what the world would say,
To lead the people all the way

Soon this babe was a young man
And he spread the Gospel all over the land
This anointing became greater now
And this great ministry was established and found.

God gave a vision for him to do
And in this vision it included you.
So this "Man of God" is unique you see,
And in God's eyes He will always have,
A love for the Word and also the task,
For he will do, whatever GOD ASK!

"DEDICATED TO DR. KENNETH PORTER"

DAUGHTHER & GRANDDAUGHTERS

Dear ones,

You have made my day

In fun, in down times and in play

Being around you ALL

Have kept me young

In laughter, in caring, in things you all have done

Life would be lonely at times you see

If there wasn't any LOVE

Between you all and me.

BROTHERS
"Jamil & Andrew"

ALWAYS TOGETHER...NEVER APART

BROTHERS

"Jamil & Andrew"

Two brothers so very strong
With each other, there is no wrong

Upholding one another, with great love
For God, put you together,
It was His plan from above

For nothing can separate you two
You see Not friends or foes,
And NOT EVEN ME!

ALWAYS TOGETHER…NEVER APART

LATISHA

WHAT A SWEET YOUNG LADY YOU HAVE BECOME

LATISHA

Oh, what a sweet young lady you have become
Taking care of your daughter, working so hard,
Keeping your home, saving your money
And you are always so very funny.

You see Tish, I am so proud of you
For you have matured and you know what to do.
Blessing your mother and I when you can
It's good to see you…
Where in the world have you been?

You see I love you, and I will… all my life
So cut the cake and give me a slice!

Happy Birthday

RYESHA

THERE IS A SWEET YOUNG LADY
THAT IS IN MY LIFE
AND NO MATTER WHERE SHE IS
HER LOVE IS THE SAME
AND IF YOU'RE TRYING TO GUESS,
RYE IS HER NAME

RYESHA

There is a sweet young lady that is in my life
And no matter where she is her love is the same
And if you're trying to guess, Rye is her NAME.

Always ready to give a helping hand
And never selfish, but does all she can
When I am going through thick or thin
When I am down in sickness or pain,
She is there to help me and doesn't want FAME

I'll always be around, If you need me to be
And my prayer for you is…ETERNALLY

ABOUT THE AUTHOR

Lillian C. Gattis was born to George and Eva Cottingham on August 12, 1945, in Blackbird, Delaware. My birth name was Lily Cottingham. I was the 6th out of the 7 children that are still living. I have 7 brothers and sisters that proceeded in death before I was born.

As a young teenager, I was introduced to Islam by my late husband, Andrew M. Clayton, Sr., in which I was taught a lot of respect and discipline. In 1980, I gave my life to Christ and was filled with His precious Holy Ghost. I am so grateful to the Lord for giving me a second chance to live because I was spiritually dead.

I can never, never forget my Pastor for his many hours of sacrifice and prayers that he has given to me and my family. My goal in life is to love God's people, to stay focused and to win souls to Christ.

www.ingramcontent.com/pod-product-compliance
Lightning Source LLC
LaVergne TN
LVHW041541060526
838200LV00037B/1079